T0400526

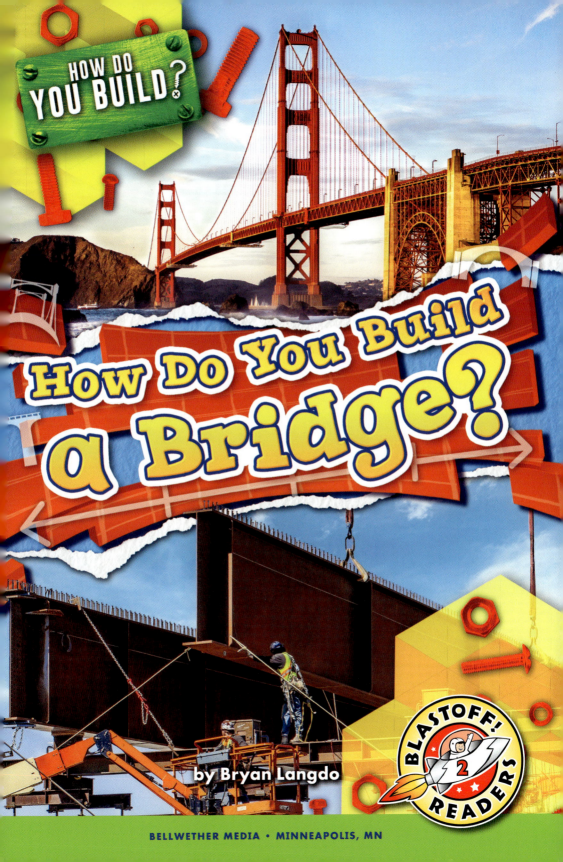

HOW DO YOU BUILD?

How Do You Build a Bridge?

by Bryan Langdo

BELLWETHER MEDIA • MINNEAPOLIS, MN

Blastoff! Readers are carefully developed by literacy experts to build reading stamina and move students toward fluency by combining standards-based content with developmentally appropriate text.

Level 1 provides the most support through repetition of high-frequency words, light text, predictable sentence patterns, and strong visual support.

Level 2 offers early readers a bit more challenge through varied sentences, increased text load, and text-supportive special features.

Level 3 advances early-fluent readers toward fluency through increased text load, less reliance on photos, advancing concepts, longer sentences, and more complex special features.

★ **Blastoff! Universe**

Reading Level

Grade **K**

Grades **1–3**

Grade **4**

This edition first published in 2026 by Bellwether Media, Inc.

No part of this publication may be reproduced in whole or in part without written permission of the publisher. For information regarding permission, write to Bellwether Media, Inc., Attention: Permissions Department, 3500 American Blvd W, Suite 150, Bloomington, MN 55431.

Library of Congress Cataloging-in-Publication Data

LC record for How Do You Build a Bridge? available at: https://lccn.loc.gov/2025010704

Text copyright © 2026 by Bellwether Media, Inc. BLASTOFF! READERS and associated logos are trademarks and/or registered trademarks of Bellwether Media, Inc. Bellwether Media is a division of FlutterBee Education Group.

Editor: Rachael Barnes   Book Designer: Josh Brink

Printed in the United States of America, North Mankato, MN.

Table of Contents

A Way Across

Cars zoom down a road.
A river lies up ahead.
But the road does not end.

A bridge lets the cars
cross safely!

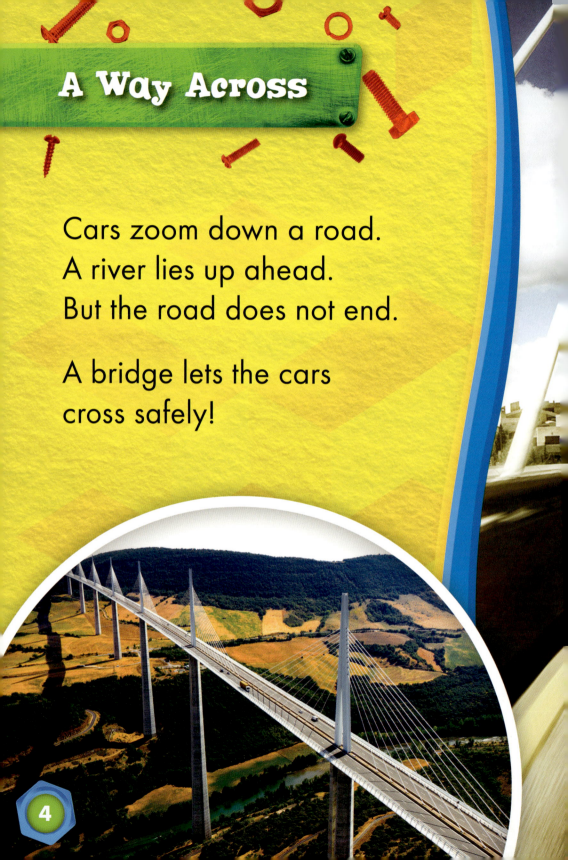

Planning a Bridge

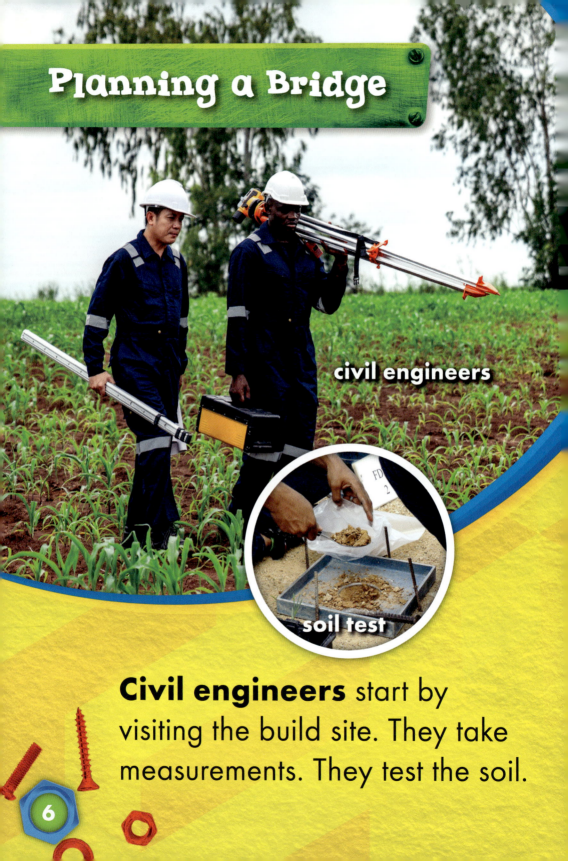

civil engineers

soil test

Civil engineers start by visiting the build site. They take measurements. They test the soil.

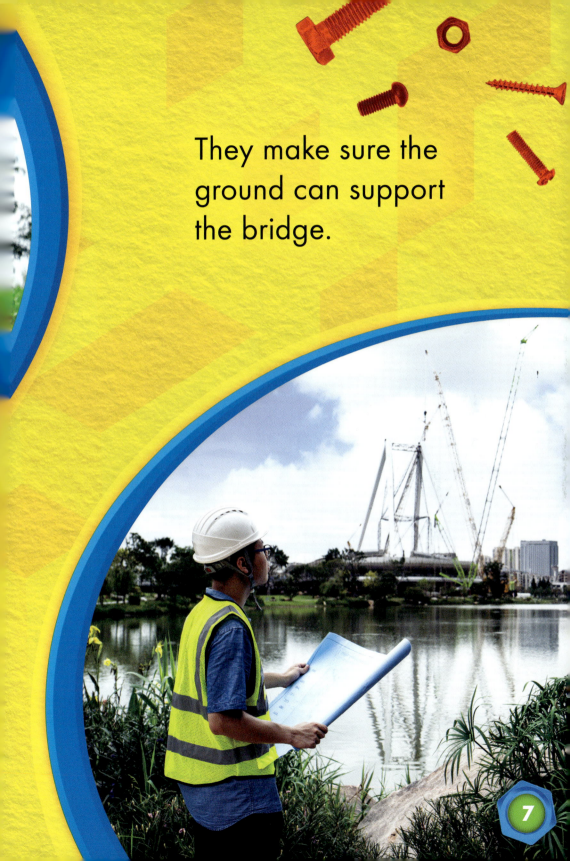

They make sure the ground can support the bridge.

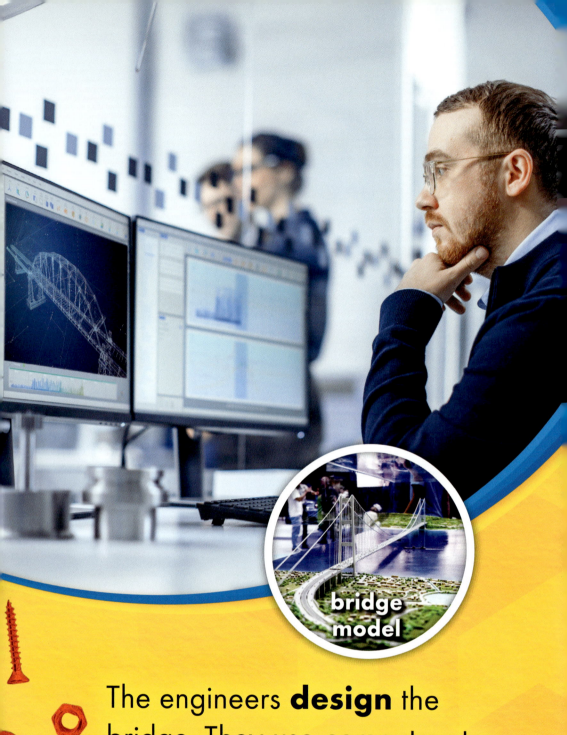

bridge model

The engineers **design** the bridge. They use computers to draw plans and make **models**.

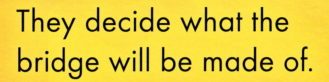

They decide what the
bridge will be made of.

What Do You Need?

steel

concrete

asphalt

Building Begins

Machines flatten the land. Next, workers begin on the bridge **foundation**.

Piles go deep into the soil. Workers pour **concrete** to form **piers** and **abutments**.

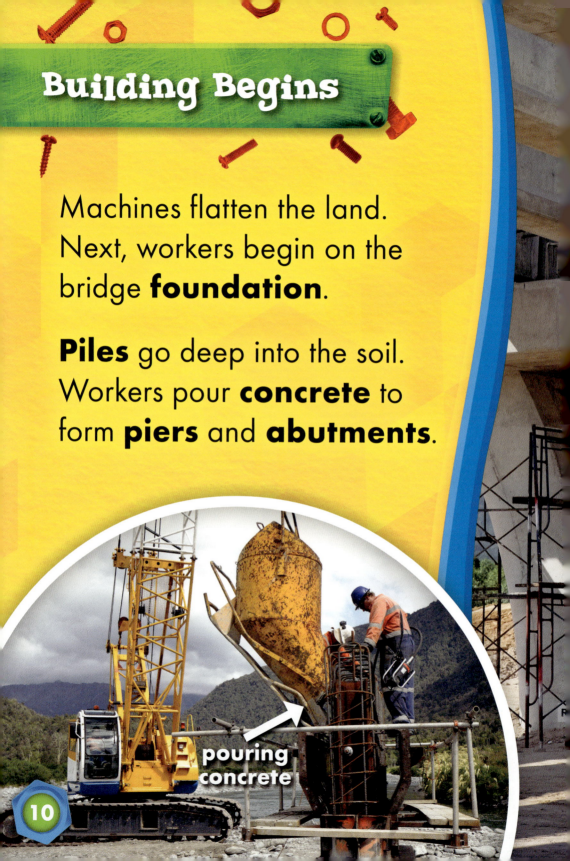

pouring concrete

pier

abutment

11

girder

Cranes lift **girders**. They place the girders across the piers and abutments.

Workers join the girders to the foundation.

Parts of a Bridge

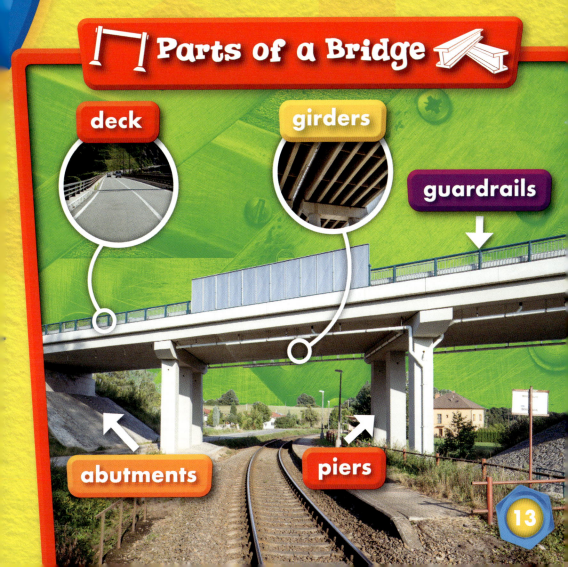

deck

girders

guardrails

abutments

piers

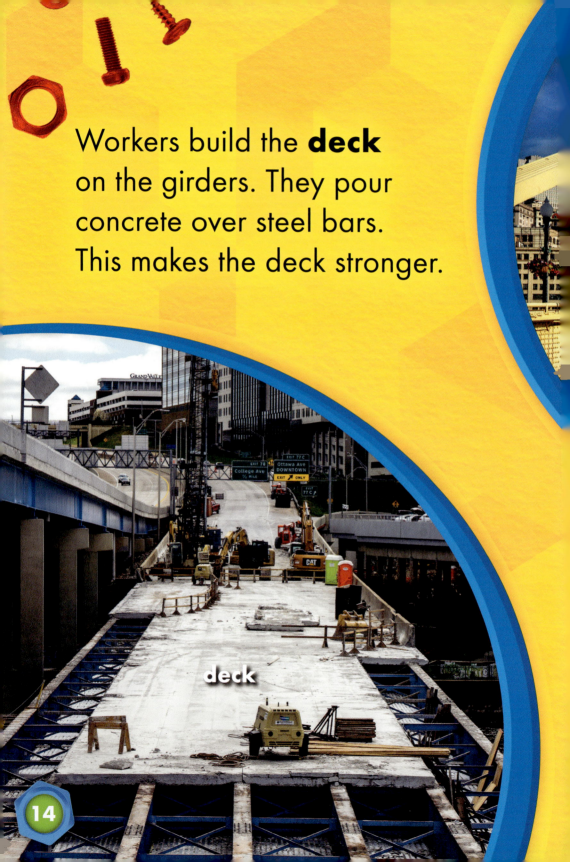

Workers build the **deck** on the girders. They pour concrete over steel bars. This makes the deck stronger.

deck

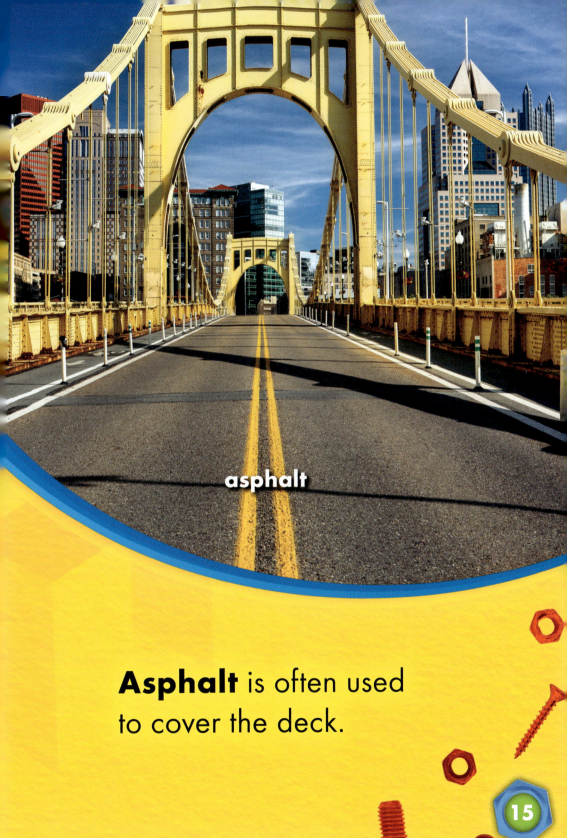

asphalt

Asphalt is often used to cover the deck.

15

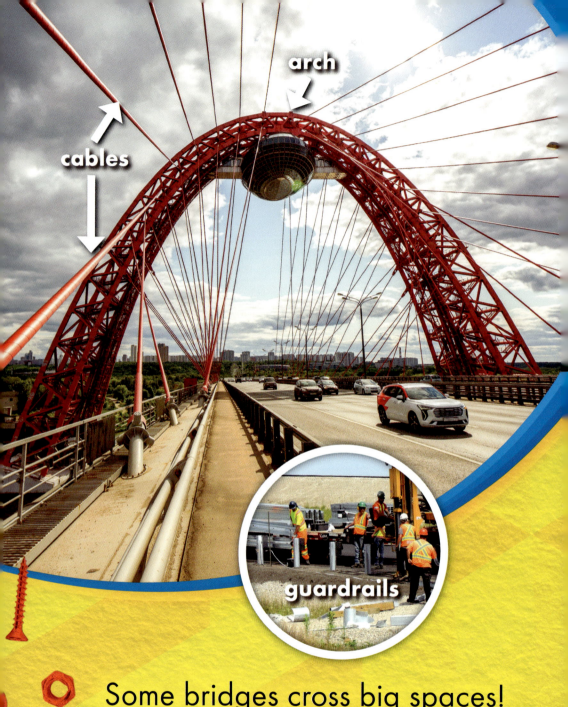

arch

cables

guardrails

Some bridges cross big spaces! They are finished with arches or cables for extra support.

Workers add **guardrails** and lights. Steel bridges get painted.

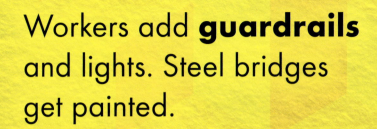

Danyang-Kunshan Grand Bridge

Location connects Shanghai and Nanjing, two major cities in China

Length 102.4 miles (164.8 kilometers)

Cost about $8.5 billion

Famous for longest bridge in the world

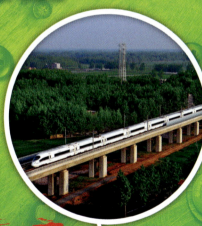

17

Inspectors make sure the finished bridge is safe.

1. Engineers visit the build site.

2. Workers take site measurements.

3. Piles go into the ground.

4. Workers build piers and abutments.

5. Workers build the bridge deck.

6. Inspectors check the bridge.

They check most bridges at least every two years. Workers fix old or broken parts.

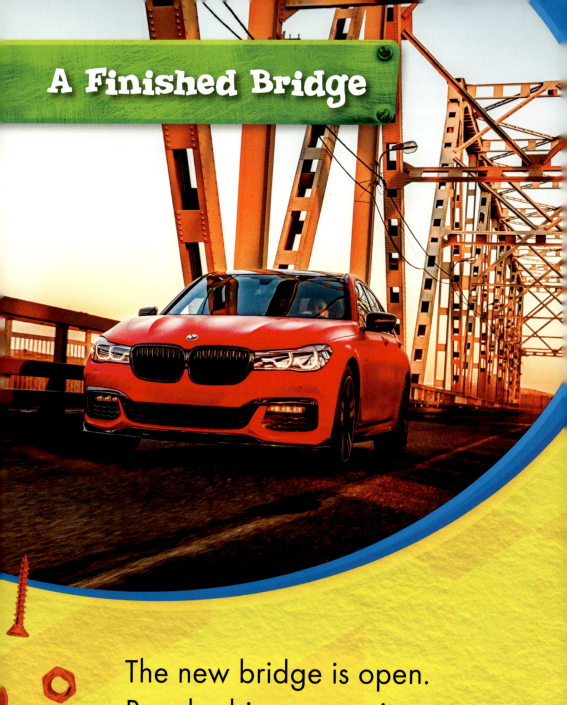

A Finished Bridge

The new bridge is open.
People drive across it
to get to work or school.

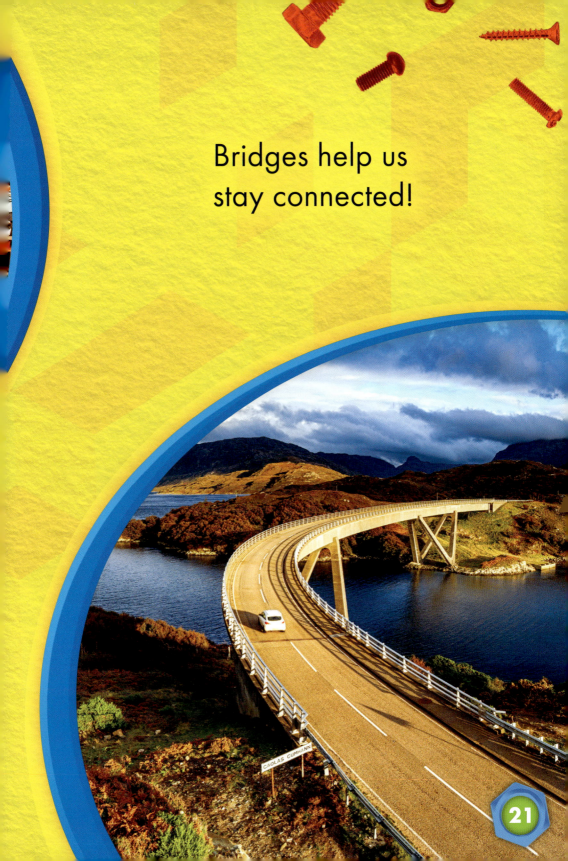

Bridges help us
stay connected!

21

Glossary

abutments—structures at either end of a bridge that hold its weight

asphalt—a hard building material made of dark sand and gravel

civil engineers—designers and builders of structures such as bridges, roads, and tunnels

concrete—a hard, strong building material made with cement, sand, rocks, and water

deck—the surface on a bridge where cars and people travel

design—to make a plan for building a bridge or other structure

foundation—a base or support on top of which a structure is built

girders—horizontal beams; girders can be made of steel or concrete.

guardrails—barriers along the sides of roads and bridges that keep people and vehicles safe

inspectors—people who check to make sure work was done correctly

models—small versions of bridges or other structures; models can be physical or digital.

piers—vertical structures that support a bridge

piles—long columns that go into the ground and help support big structures

To Learn More

AT THE LIBRARY

Agrawal, Roma. *How Was That Built? The Stories Behind Awesome Structures.* New York, N.Y.: Bloomsbury Children's Books, 2022.

Holdren, Annie C. *Building the Golden Gate Bridge.* Mankato, Minn.: Amicus, 2023.

Majewski, Marc. *Bridges.* New York, N.Y.: Abrams Books for Young Readers, 2023.

ON THE WEB

Factsurfer.com gives you a safe, fun way to find more information.

1. Go to www.factsurfer.com.

2. Enter "bridge" into the search box and click 🔍.

3. Select your book cover to see a list of related content.

Index

The images in this book are reproduced through the courtesy of: ju.hrozian, cover (top hero); Randy Hergenrether, cover (bottom hero), p. 12; SvetlanaSF, pp. 2-3; BearFotos, p. 4; Ayman alakhras, pp. 4-5; NewJadsada, p. 6; noramin.s, p. 6 (soil test); xiaoke chen/ Getty Images, p. 7; Gorodenkoff, p. 8; Independent Photo Agency Srl/ Alamy, p. 8 (bridge model); saweang.w, p. 9 (steel); ungvar, p. 9 (concrete); Ba_peuceta, p. 9 (asphalt); Lakeview Images, p. 10; Macharoenwong Angkana, pp. 10-11, 19 (step four); Korekore, p. 13 (deck); Michal, p. 13 (bridge); ASGOLD, p. 13 (girder); Ayman Haykal, p. 14; Aevan, p. 15; Osiev, p. 16; hilmver, p. 16 (guardrails); Imaginechina/ Alamy, p. 17; Siwawut Phoophinyo, pp. 18-19; kanpisut, p. 19 (step one); Chalermwoot, p. 19 (step two); Navokifaut, p. 19 (step three); Alexey Savchuk, p. 19 (step five); Monty Rakusen/ Getty Images, p. 19 (step six); Roman, p. 20; Helen Hotson, p. 21; dvoevnore, pp. 22-23; Dario, p. 23.